Romance Variations

Guitar Solo

I0792709

by Rico Stover

Audio Contents

1	Romance Variations as one through track [12:01]
2	Introduction [0:00-0:22]
3	Romance Theme [0:23-1:21]
4	Variation 1: Arpegiado [1:22-2:21]
5	Variation 2: Bordoneo [2:22-3:42]
6	Variation 3: Villa-Lobosiana [3:44-5:23]
7	Variation 4: Bossanova [5:24-6:51]
8	Variation 5: Chet's Pick [6:52-8:05]
9	Variation 6: Aire de Danza part 1 [8:06-10:05]
10	Variation 6: Aire de Danza part 2 [10:06-10:32]
11	Variation 6: Aire de Danza part 3 [10:33-12:01]

1 2

Visit us on the Web at www.melbay.com — E-mail us at email@melbay.com

Dedicated to my mother Lois, who loved the *Romance*.

Table of Contents

Romance Anónimo 5
Arpegiado 8
Bordoneo 11
Villa-Lobosiana 13
Bossanova 16
Chet's Pick 19
Aire de Danza 22

Who Composed the *Romance Anónimo*? 30
Romance Anónimo music examples/analysis 35
"*Estudio*" edition circa 1900 39

Variations on *Romance Anónimo*

Track 1

This composition is comprised of six variations on the universally popular work known as *Anonymous Romance* (a.k.a. *Spanish Romance, Romance de Amor, Estudio de Rubira, Jeux Interdits*). I have composed six variations using as my inspiration guitarists from former eras: Luis Milan, Mateo Carcassi, Heitor Villa-Lobos, Atahualpa Yupanqui, Luíz Bonfá, Joe Pass and Chet Atkins-a tapestry of guitar styles woven into a theme and variations of twelve minutes duration.

Introduction
The *Romance* is written in 3/4 meter and the melody is written as quarter notes. The opening two measure phrase of descending notes is a rhythmic motif that appears throughout the work in different forms. It is announced in the *Introduction* with different key centers in rapid succession, resolving to the dominant of the key of e minor, setting the stage for the work itself.

Main Theme
The *Romance* is 32 measures in length, with 16 measures in e minor and 16 measures in the parallel major key of E. The version featured here utilizes the right hand fingering pattern of a-m-i articulating triplets on each beat.

Variation 1: *Arpegiado*
Arpeggios are the concept behind this first variation, utilizing primarily a-m-i-p-i-m with alterations. The theme is extended and elongated as it is heard over a rapidly executed arpeggio underpinning.

Variation 2: *Bordoneo*
In Spanish the bass strings are called *bordones* and thus the word "bordoneo" refers to "bass string playing". The minor key variation utilizes the technique of *basso ostinato*, after which the major key section proceeds with a "walking bass" pattern typical of popular music and jazz.

Variation 3: *Villa–Lobosiana*
This variation draws its inspiration from the guitar works of the Brazilian composer Heitor Villa-Lobos utilizing open strings, diminished seventh chords, harmonics, dramatic effects, etc.

Variation 4: *Bossanova*
A syncopated variation in the harmonic and rhythmic style of the popular Brazilian form that draws its inspiration from Luíz Bonfá, A.C. Jobim and Baden Powell.

Variation 5: *Chet's Pick*
Inspired by the great Chet Atkins, this variation utilizes a traditional "fingerpicking" concept with a decidedly "country/folk" flavor.

Variation 6: *Aire de Danza*
This variation employs the 3/4-6/8 feeling that pervades much of Latin American music. The style here derives its inspiration from the great Argentine *guitarristas criollos* (creole guitarists) Eduardo Falú and Atahualpa Yupanqui. The theme is treated in a variety of key centers and textures with an unrelenting and intense rhythmic pulse, punctuated by a slow lyrical section that appears briefly and then returns to the frenetic pulse of the *danza*, leading to a coda section that culminates in an orgy of rasgueado strumming.

Track 2

Romance Anónimo

Theme and Variations

Rico Stover

Introduction

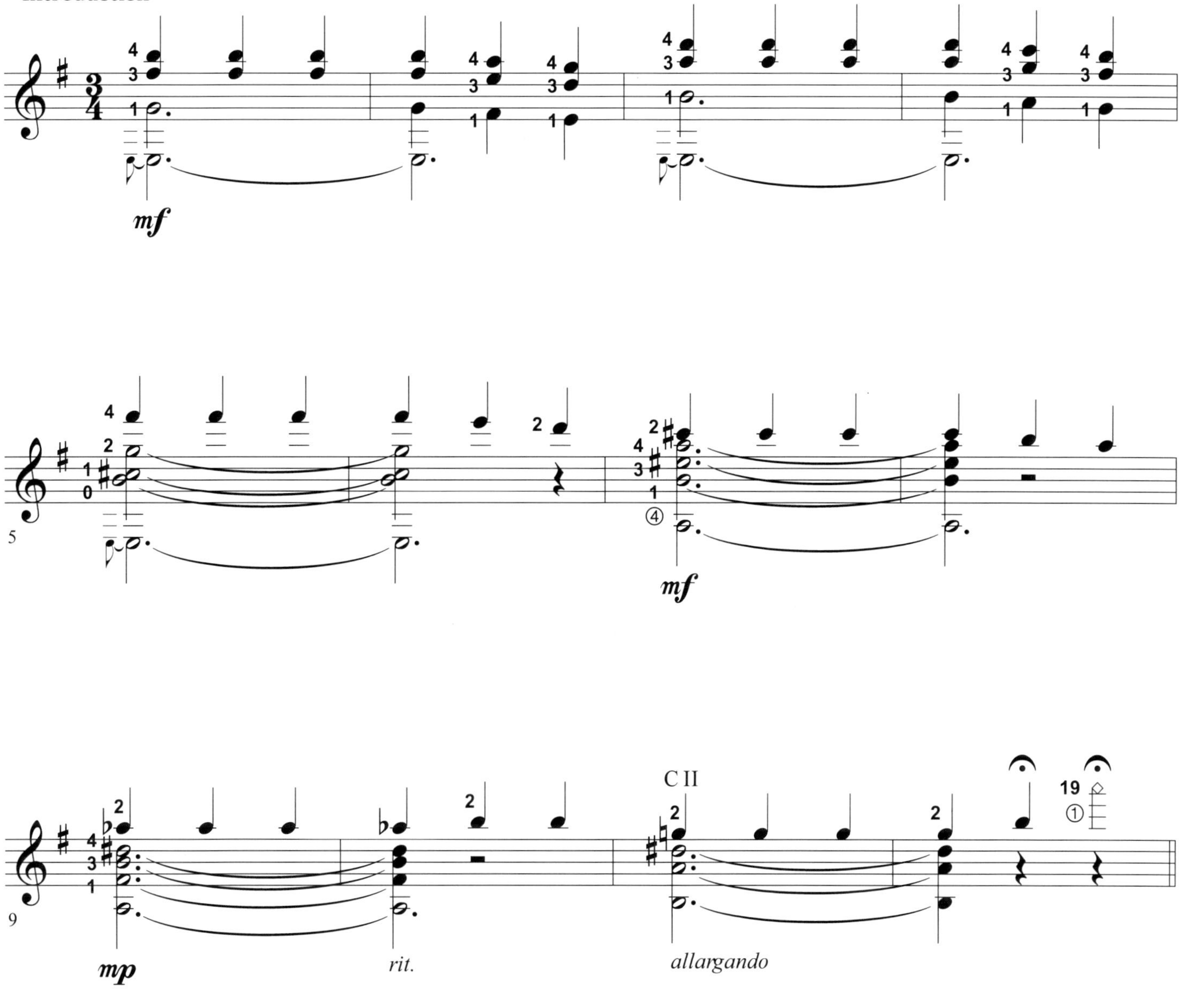

Track 3

Theme

C II
29
C VII
32
C IX
C IX
35
C V
C V
38
C II
41
43

Track 4

Arpegiado

Variation 1

Romance Variations

C II
C II
rit.
p
C VII
C VII
C VII
C IV
poco rit.
accelerando

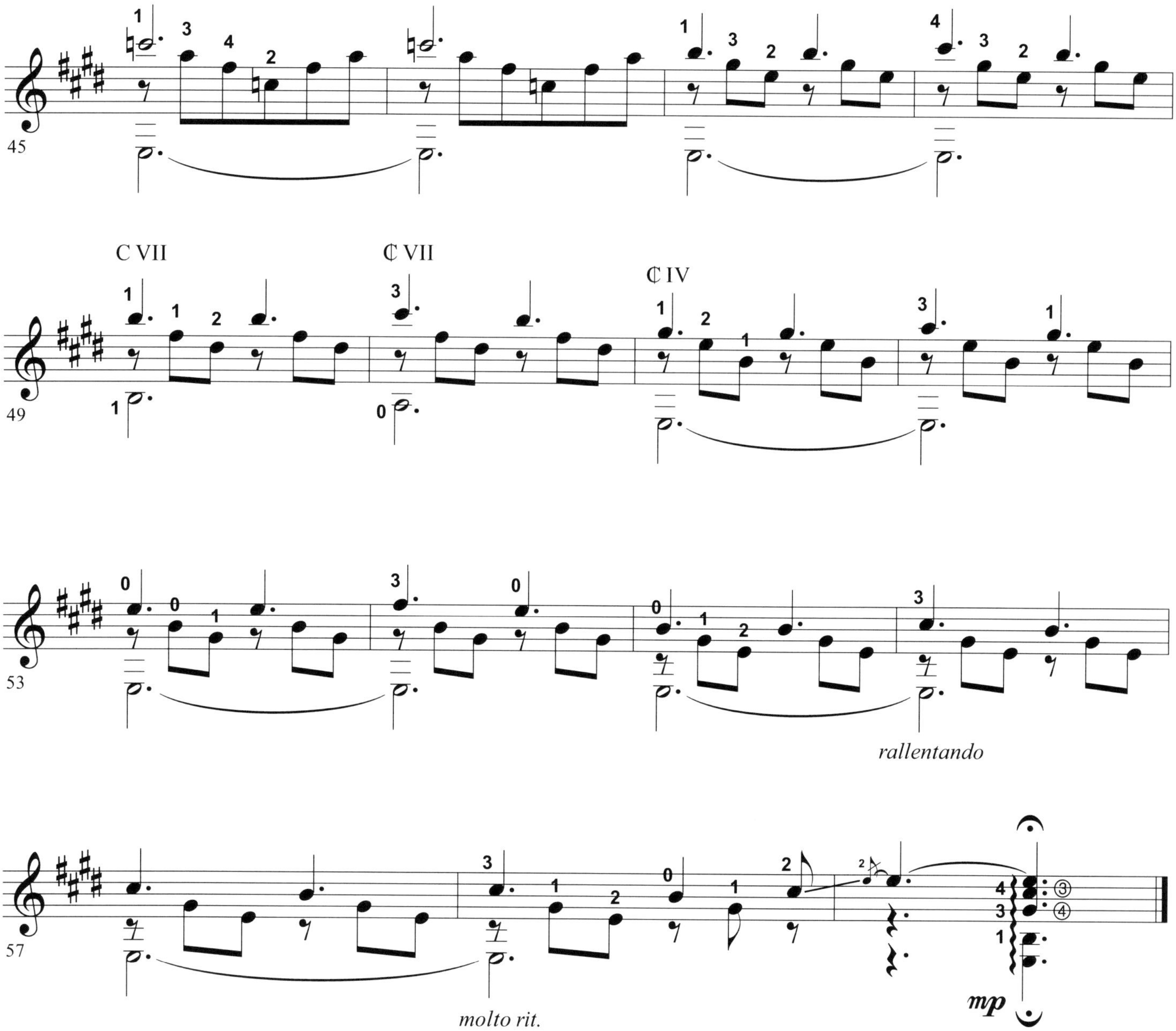
45
C VII
₵ VII
₵ IV
49
53
rallentando
57
molto rit.
mp

Track 5

Bordoneo

Variation 2

Romance Variations

♩. = 80 - 84

♩= 138
briskly
walking bass
C II
C IV
gliss.
pizz.
C IV
C II
normale
p

Villa-Lobosiana

Variation 3

Track 6

Romance Variations

♩ = 96 - 100

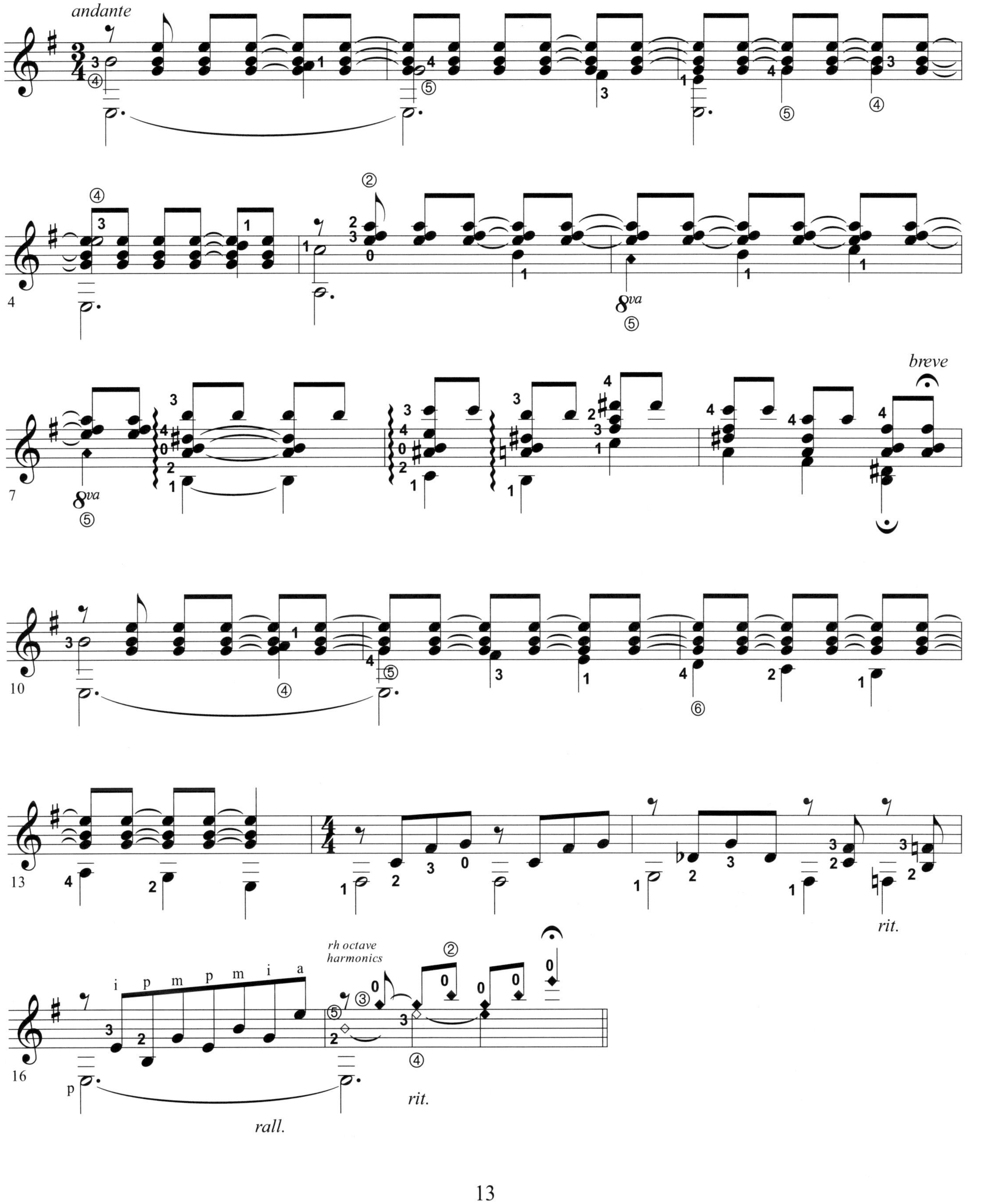

♩= 88 - 92
p
p
rallentando
rit.

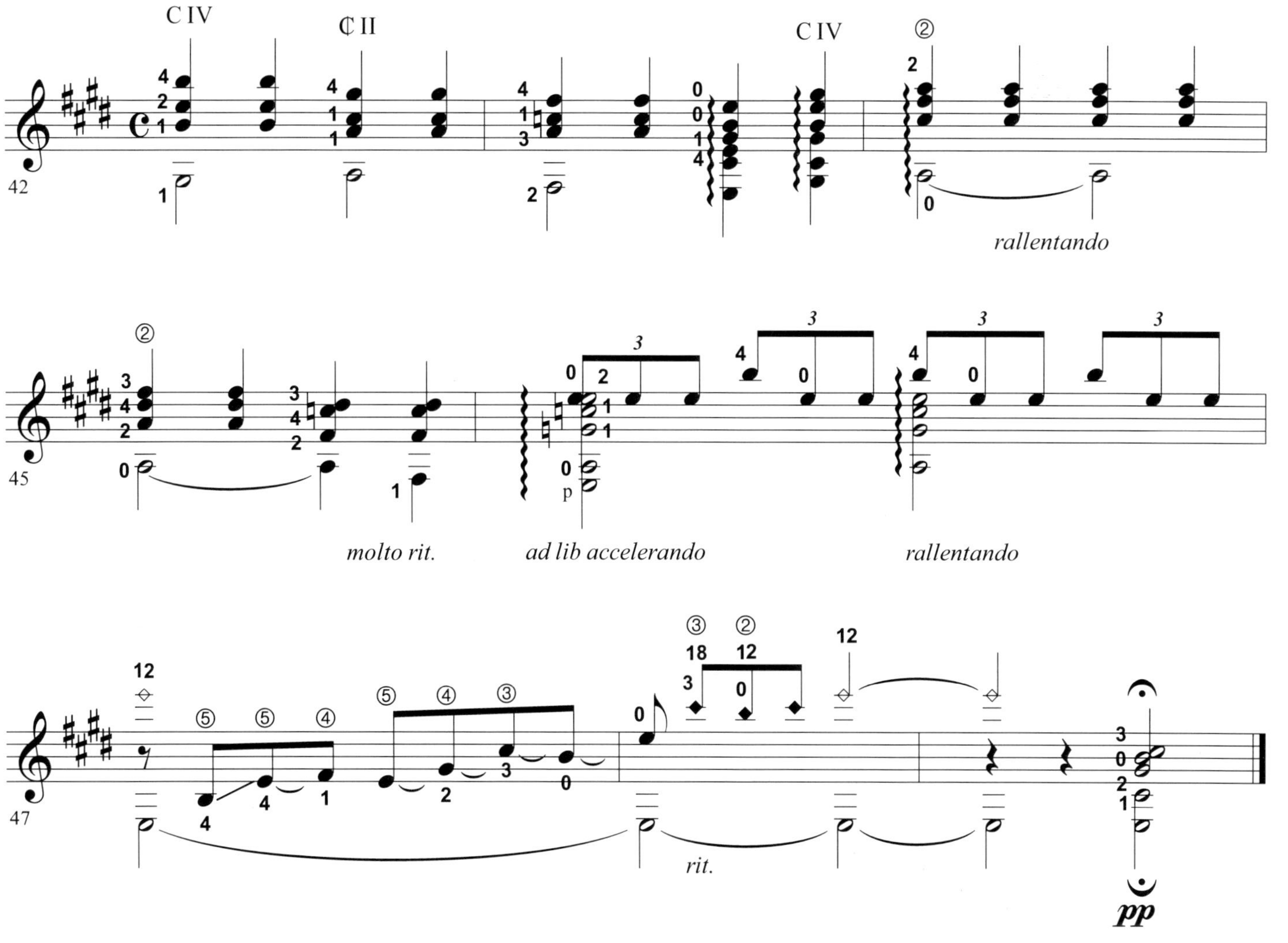
C IV
₵ II
C IV
rallentando
molto rit.
ad lib accelerando
rallentando
rit.
pp

Track 7

Bossanova

Variation 4

Romance Variations

25
29
gliss.
C IV
33
C IV
C III
37
41
C VII
C VII
C VII

C VII
C V
C V
C III
C II
poco rall.
harms. naturales 5th
p

Track 8

Chet's Pick

Variation 5

Romance Variations

C VII
25
29
33
37
C I
41
45
49
C V

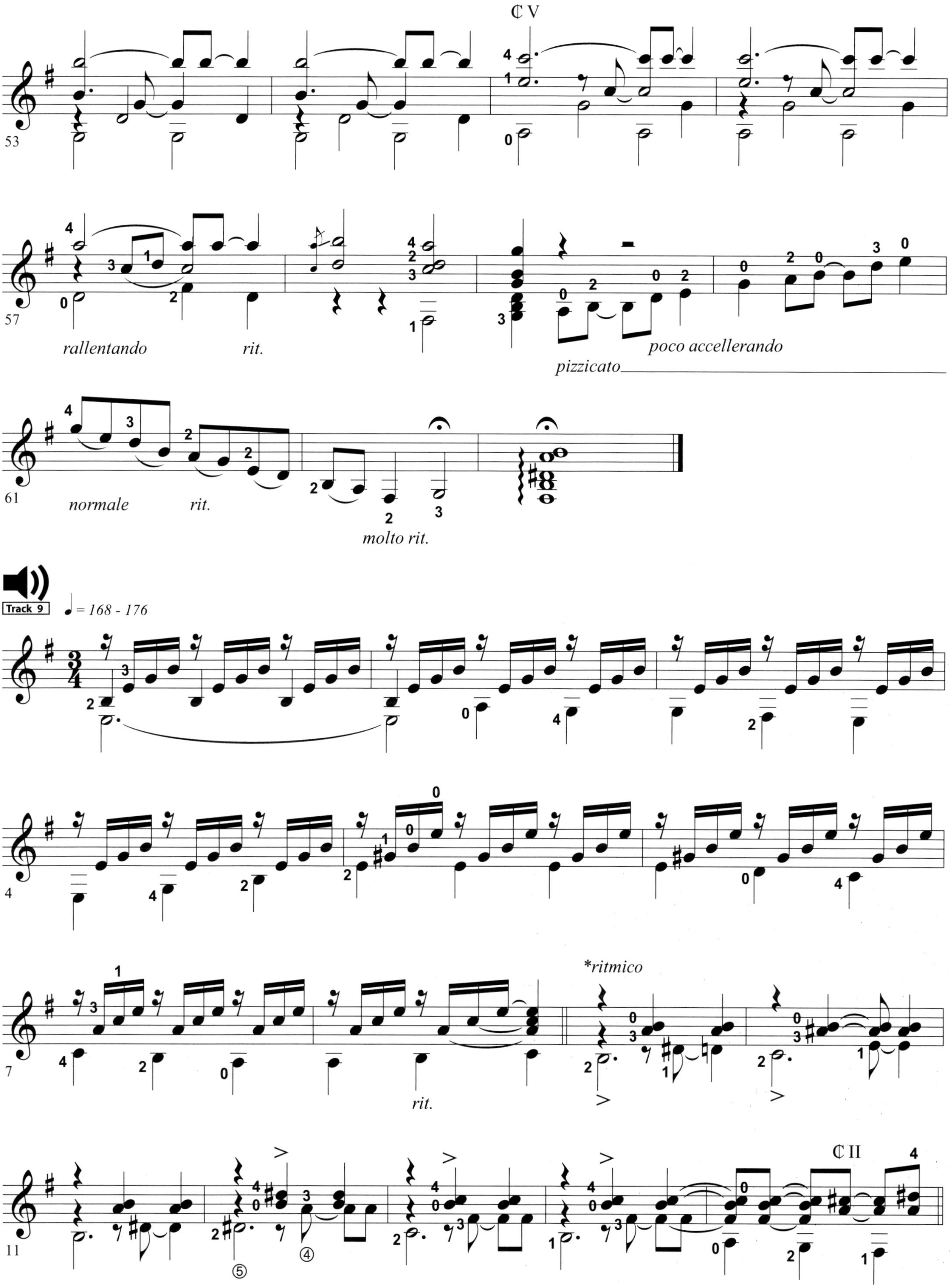

*gradually increase tempo to ♩ = *176 - 184* for *Aire de Danza*

Track 9

Aire de Danza

Variation 6

Romance Variations

♩ = 176 - 184

*Denotes a *golpe* with left side of thumb.

C II
C II
C II
C II
C IV
C II
C I

C II
C VII
C VII
C VII
C VII
C VII
C II
ff
C II
C II

C IV
C VII
C IV
C II
C IV
C II
poco rit.
rall.
breve

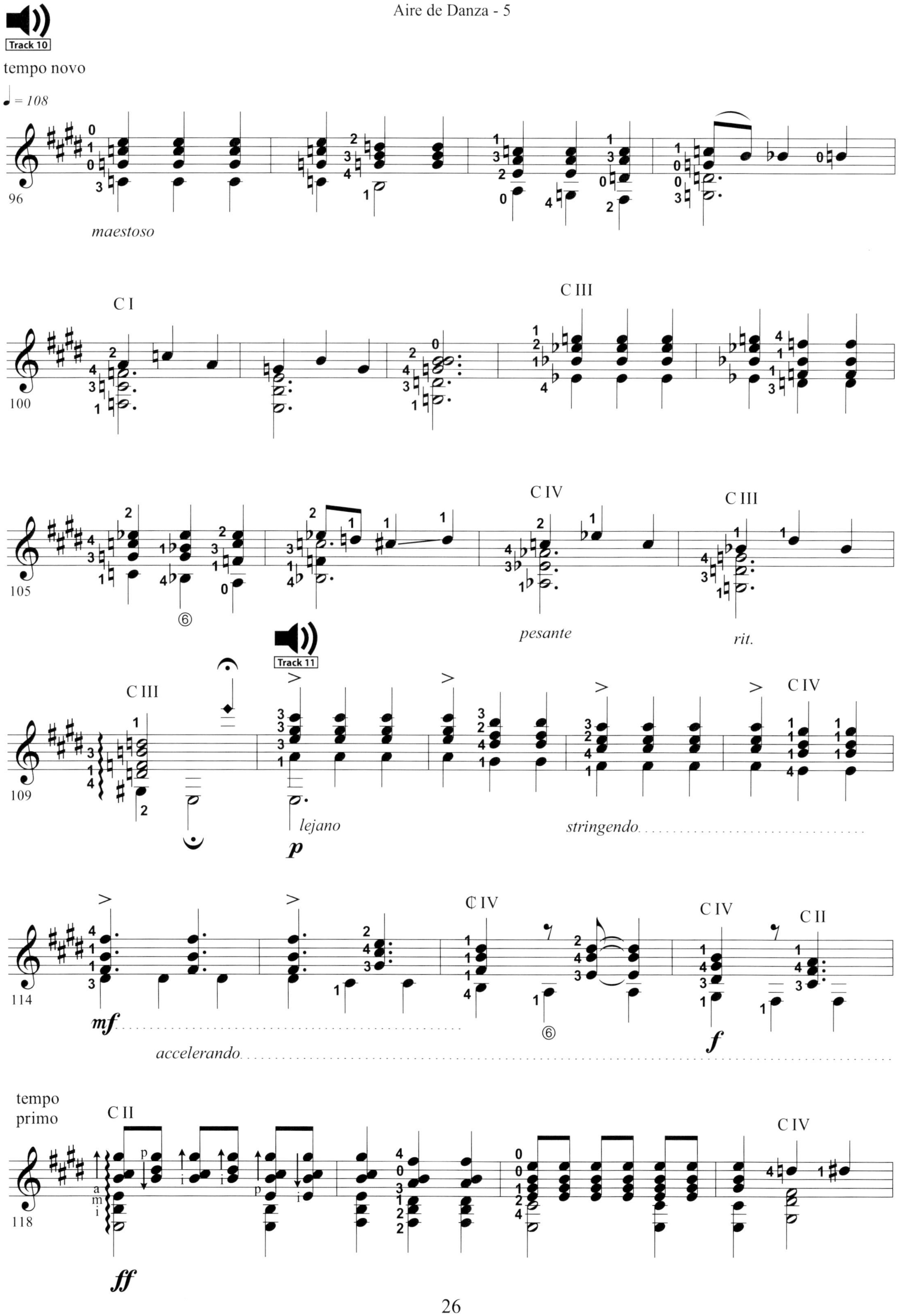
Track 10
tempo novo
♩ = 108
96
maestoso
C I
C III
100
C IV
C III
105
pesante
rit.
Track 11
C III
109
lejano
p
stringendo
C IV
114
mf
accelerando
C IV
C IV
C II
f
tempo primo
C II
118
ff
C IV

C II
C I
C II
C VII
C VII
C VII
C VII
C VII
C II
a
m
i
p
ff
ff

C II
C II
f
₵ IV
C VII
ff
₵ IV
₵ II
fff
ff
pesante
allargando
molto

C II
167
molto rit.
tenuto
a tempo
C II
171
allargando
molto rit.
tenuto
ff
C IV
C II
175
allargando
rit.
rallentando
C I
179
molto rit.
f
183
ff
mp

Who Composed the "Romance Anónimo?"

by Rico Stover with Randy Osborne

"The popularity of the 'Romance'...is justified by the tranquil beauty of the piece, by its fluency on the instrument for which it was written."

Isaias Savio, 1966

"One of the most-published and most-played pieces...Such popularity, naturally, means that it is widely shunned by serious guitarists. But who actually wrote it?"

David Grimes, 1988

During my first year of studying guitar (1962) my teacher gave me the "Romance Anónimo" in a publication by the Spanish guitarist Vicente Gomez.[1] I liked it immediately because it was not all that difficult and also, once I could play it at a decent tempo, I noticed that people really liked it (especially my mother). Fifty years later I still play this "magical arpeggio study" which continues to enjoy universal popularity all around the world.

But the question of who composed this work remains unanswered. Though there are many contenders, to date no irrefutable evidence to prove the identity of the composer has been found and the question thus remains open. The different theories[2] regarding this mystery boil down to:

1. **Fernando Sor** is the composer according to Francisco Herrera who cites a manuscript with the title "*Melodía de Sor*", plus a cylinder recording labelled "Sort-Estudio para Guitarra".
2. **Antonio Rubira** is the composer according to quotes from Prat, and a manuscript with the title "*Estudio de Don Antonio Rubira*".
3. **Francisco Tárrega** is the composer according to Soares.
4. **David del Castillo** is the composer according to the Dotras family.
5. **Pedro Maza** is the composer according to his publication.
6. **Daniel Fortea** is the composer according to his publication.
7. **Vicente Gomez** is the composer according to his publication.
8. **Narciso Yepes** is the composer according to his publication.

Recent evidence corroborates that an edition of this work was edited around 1900.[3] As a consequence of this verification, the claims by all those in the 20th century become invalid. That leaves Sor, Tárrega, Antonio Rubira and David del Castillo on the list of contenders for the title of "Composer of the Romance."

One other fanciful explanation offered by Angelo Gilardino attributes the work to the flamenco master Francisco Rodríguez "El Murciano" (1795-1848) with whom the Russian composer Mikhail Glinka (1804-1857) spent several years in Spain attempting to transcribe the *falsetas* of the flamenco master. Gilardino states that he saw "in a vision" Glinka trying to play a Russian melody of his youth on El Murciano's guitar. Not being a guitarist, Glinka could only play the melody he loved note by note on the first string. As he attempted to play the melody, El Murciano, after listening, took the guitar and instantly captured the melody, rendering it in a form similar to what we know today.

Of course, this is all fantasy but there might be a grain of truth in it. Perhaps El Murciano did elaborate on the motif and compose the work. He was not a literate musician so if he did compose it then it had to have been transferred to others first hand with no manuscript involved. This would of course have been in the three years when Glinka was in Spain preceding El Murciano's death in 1848. Perhaps the work entered into the popular guitar tradition "by ear" and Antonio Rubira heard it around 1860? I ask myself this: why is there a question regarding the authorship? Is it perhaps because Rubira learned the work by ear in his youth and never really felt he could legitimately take credit for it? Being a literate musician, he could have written it out for his guitarist friends, who included prominent players of the era such as Juan Parga, who in turn wrote it out for others, beginning a tradition of hand copied manuscripts.

This is perhaps one reason as to why there was no formally published edition of the work in Spain during the period 1850-1929. But proof that the work existed and was played in Spain during the latter decades of the 19th century also comes from a wax cylinder recording dated c. 1900 from Madrid featuring guitarist Simon Ramirez playing the *Romance*. This cylinder is labelled "*Sort: Estudio para Guitarra*" and was made on a cylinder of the Viuda de Aramburo company. It is assumed that "Sort" here is a misnomer for Sor.

And what about Sor? The case for Sor as made by the Spanish musicologist Francisco Herrera rests on the presentation of a handwritten manuscript of the work with the title "*Melodia de Sor.*" No date. According to its owner José María Lopez de la Osa of Madrid, this manuscript is from the 19th century, having been part of the archives of the Spanish guitarist Daniel Fortea, who published a version in 1930 through his Biblioteca Fortea editorial. The other piece of evidence is the cylinder recording labeled "Sort: Estudio para Guitarra" mentioned above. Herrera closes his argument with the statement "Why couldn't F. Sor be the composer of such a beautiful melody?" As Porras points out, Sor's music is contrapuntal and polyphonic and in his opinion the structure of the *Romance* does not fit this mold. I concur with Porras and have to add that once you have studied enough of Sor's works you will quite probably concur. Perhaps the "melody" of the first part is something Sor heard during his travels in Russia and brought back with him in some form? This is doubtful, but still something to think about.

The evidence for Antonio Rubira is circumstantial, most of it coming from Domingo Prat in his *Diccionario de Guitarristas*. There are three references to Antonio Rubira in Prat (pages 74, 153 and 274). In addition there are two references to Antonio Rovira (pages 126 and 297). On page 297 Prat states: "…tal estudio pertenece a Antonio Rovira, y fué en el año 1876 copiado por Juan Parga para la hija del guitarrista Juan Valler que actuara en Buenos Aires…". ("This study belongs to Antonio Rovira, and it was copied in the year 1876 by Juan Parga for the daughter of the guitarist Juan Valler, who would be active in Buenos Aires"). It must be noted that Antonio Rovira and Antonio Rubira are not the same person but two distinct Spanish musicians born in the first half of the 19th century.[4] The fact is that Prat erroneously refers to "Rovira" as being the author of the "*Estudio*," when he means Rubira. However, in the entry for the Barcelona musician José Ferrés on page 126, Prat refers to Ferrés as being an "artistic grandfather" to *Rovira*, which is in fact correct. As the name Rovira was seen on the first printed edition of the work from Buenos Aires (of which Prat was no doubt aware), he may have thought it simply a misnomer.

I believe that Parga, Valler and Rubira knew one another and that they all were familiar with the work in question. Prat affirms on page 327 that Juan Valler (1835-1926) knew a great many of the prominent guitarists of mid 19th century Spain: "…he knew Huerta, Carnicer, Muro, A. Cano, Arcas…" To this must be added guitarists in Argentina that Valler came to know in the 48 years that he lived in Buenos Aires. So the connection between Argentina and the *Romance* in all probability has a great deal to do with Juan Valler, the Spanish guitarist born in Andalucia in 1835 who immigrated to Argentina[5] in 1878 and who functioned as a great fount of information for Domingo Prat for nearly three decades (proof of this is the fact that Valler is mentioned a total of 19 times by Prat in his *Diccionario*).

Another piece of pro-Rubira evidence is a handwritten manuscript with the title "Estudio de Don Antonio Rubira." Antonio Company, the owner of this manuscript, claims that it dates from "the last part of the 19th century" with no specific date. Another handwritten manuscript in Company's possession is a "*Mazurka*" by Rubira. This information is from Francisco Herrera in his *Enciclopedia de la Guitarra* on page 2296. In the area of formally published works, Rubira was active in Madrid with three different editorials: the Antonio Romero y Andía editorial which published a transcription of the Sinfonía from the opera "Nabucodonosor" (Verdi), a Tango from the zarzuela "Marina" and an original work *El Aniversario* (waltz); with the Vicente Enrique Abad Editorial in 1878 he published his "Valses Fantásticos" and in 1880 with Faustino Echevarría Editorial he published *Marcha de los Cadetes*, as well as *Mandolinata – Recuerdos de Roma* (Paladilhe). In 1872 he offered a music publication by subscription which featured in each issue "a work from an opera correctly written and perfectly arranged, plus one original work."[6] Seeing as how Rubiano was active in publishing, one wonders why he did not publish his popular *Estudio*.

Rubira was evidently an accomplished and refined player whom Prat called "the very cultured Spanish guitarist" (page 74) and whom the *Diccionario de la musica española e hispanoamericana* described on page 457 as a guitarist of "finesse and taste" with original works that were "presented with great effect and mastery…" Julian Arcas (1832-1882) and Juan Parga (1843-1899) were "devoted admirers" of Rubira "attracted by the sublimity of his pulsation" who "believed that they had discovered in this artist a supernatural talent." (Prat, page 274).

As concerns the argument that Francisco Tárrega composed the work, the source of this claim comes from a method for guitar titled *A Escola de Tárrega* published in Brazil by Oswaldo Soares in 1929. In this method the *Romance* is shown on page 20 as "Estudo em Mi Menor." Soares attributes the music to Francisco Tárrega as an "unedited work" but offers no evidence to prove this claim. Curiosly enough, this version has two measures expunged from the score-ms. 10 and ms. 28.

The claim that the guitarist David del Castillo (1850?-1939) is the composer of the *Romance* comes from a French guitarist/pianist named Joan Dotras who in an article on the internet on the site www.guitarra.artepulsado.com* asserts that David del Castillo was a friend of Fernando Sor who fled Spain with Sor in 1813. But doing the math, Porras states that the David del Castillo referred to by Dotras as the author of the *Romance* has to be the son (or grandson) of the David del Castillo who was a contemporary of Sor in the early 19th century. But the connection between young del Castillo II (or III) and Sor is interesting. Did Sor play this melody for del Castillo Sr. who passed it on to his son/grandson? Prat documents David del Castillo in four entries, stating that he was a friend and contemporary of Antonio Jimenez Manjón (1866-1919) and that he resided in Paris for many decades. One of the last things this Spanish guitarist did was to locate the tomb of Fernando Sor in Paris. Dotras presents no evidence and as such the assertion that the Spanish guitarist David del Castillo is the author of the work is doubtful. (*www.guitarra.artepulsado.com/guitarra/viejo_ariculo_romance_%20anonimo.htm).

In analyzing these different explanations, I would rate the probability factor for each assertion as follows: a low probability for Sor; a medium high probability for Rubira; a doubtful probability for El Murciano and David del Castillo and no probability whatsoever for Tárrega. It is not possible to conclude with certainty at this time who composed the *Romance*, but if I were a betting man, I would put my money on Antonio Rubira.

I concur with Savio that the popularity of this work is due to its musical appeal and its naturalness on the instrument. But a third reason that must be taken into account is the lack of copyright and composer royalties. If no author can be claimed, then publishing becomes less problematic and more potentially lucrative, and this explains in part the abundant number of published versions that have appeared over the years.[7] The *Romance* is a popular work because it is not that difficult to master, it has a pleasing, soulful melody that challenges the student with vibrato, position shifting and the use of the barre, and it is in the key of E (a particularly effective acoustic reality for the instrument).

Chronology of the Romance

1800?	Melody evolves in Spain
1850?	The work is part of an aural tradition among guitarists in Spain.
1860?	Rubira writes down (composes?) the work in binary form.
1876	Parga hand copies the work for Valler's daughter.
1897/1901	Viuda de Aramuburo cylinder recording of the work
1900	Published edition by J. A. Medina e Hijo in Buenos Aires
1920	Mascaro y Reissig guitar method in Buenos Aires features the work.
1929	Oswaldo Soares publishes the work in his *A Escola de Tárrega*.
1931	Daniel Fortea edition in Spain
1932	Pedro Maza edition in *Album para Guitarra de seis piezas*
1940	Vicente Gomez publishes his version as *Romance de Amor*.
1952	Yepes' version used in the film *Jeux interdits* ("Forbidden Games")[8]
1958	Edition by Hernandez, Editorial Saraceno, Buenos Aires
1968	Miguel Llobet edition published posthumously by Union Musical Española, Madrid

Analysis of the Editions

Seven editions of the work that appeared from 1900 through 1968 are herein considered:

1. Medina e Hijo (1900), Maza (1932)
2. Soares (1929)
3. Fortea (1930), Yepes (1953), Llobet (1968)
4. Gomez (1940)
5. Hernandez (1958)
6. Manuscript 1 no date
7. Manuscript 2 no date

[1] **J. A. Medina e Hijo, 1900; Pedro Maza 1932** (Argentina)
The earliest published version yet located, it is the only version that departs from the triplet configuration, instead utilizing a sixteenth note figure employing aimi. A slight melodic variation is seen in measures 11, 12, 13 and 14 (see musical examples). The edition that Pedro Maza edited is identical to the Medina edition, except for some barre markings. From the archives of Mario Rodriguez Arenas (1879-1949) and Ricardo Muñoz (1887-1967) respectively, Buenos Aires.

[2] **Oswaldo Soares 1929** (Casa Bevilacqua-J. Carvalho & Cia., Sao Paulo, Brazil). As mentioned above, in this edition each section of the work has been shortened by one measure (measures 10 and 28 are omitted) and Tárrega is credited as the composer.

[3] **Daniel Fortea 1930** (Biblioteca Fortea, Madrid, Spain)
Identical to the versions by Llobet and Yepes.

[4] **Vicente Gomez 1940** (American Academy of Music, New York, United States)
Contains the most number of "changes" from the other versions. See musical examples.

[5] **Hernandez 1958** (Editorial Saraceno, Buenos Aires, Argentina)
Three measures have incorrect notes: measure 20 lacking a double sharp sign on C; measure 22 where C sharp on the second beat should be a D sharp; measure 26 where the melodic note should be D sharp but shows C sharp instead. Attributes the piece to "Robira." "Hernandez" is a pseudonym for Cosme Caballero, who ran the Casa Nuñez store in Buenos Aires during the 1940-50s (from the archive of José Augusto Marcellino, 1911-1970).

[6] **Manuscript 1** from Antonio Company, Spain
A handwritten manuscript that purports to be from "the late 19th century" that shows the title "*Estudio de Don Antonio Rubira*" (no date).

[7] **Manuscript 2** "*Melodía de Sor*" from Fortea archive, Spain. Handwritten manuscript that purports to be from the 19th century with the title "Melody of Sor" (no date).

ENDNOTES

1. Gomez, Vicente: *Romance de Amor*, American Academy of Music, New York, 1940.

2. In 2002 an important article appeared on the internet* by Santiago Porras Alvarez titled "What Do We Not Know about the Anonymous Romance?" (*¿Qué no sabemos del romance anónimo?*) This extensive investigation discusses the different theories regarding the identity of the composer of the *Romance*. Thanks to Porras we have a concise listing of those who have claimed to be the true composer of the work: El Murciano, Sor, Tárrega, Rubira, del Castillo, Maza, Fortea, Gomez, Yepes and Llobet. (**http://guitarra.artepulsado.com/guitarra/romance-anonimo.php#mnotal19*)

3. This edition was done by José A. Medina e Hijo, a company founded in the 1870s and which sold instruments, imported pianos and stood out as a publisher of Argentine music of all genres. Fixing the date for the edition of the *Romance* is an interpolation based on plate numbers of published works from JA Medina coordinated with advertisements of the day that appeared in the Argentine magazine *Caras y Carretas*. The plate number for "*Estudio*" by "Rovira" is 23697. An advertisement in *Caras y Carretas* dated November 15, 1902 lists a piano solo for sale with plate number 25705. The gap in numeration between these two editions indicates that from the time the *Estudio* by Rovira was published up until late 1902, the firm had issued a total of 2008 editions. This in fact may indicate that the *Estudio* was edited even earlier than 1900.

4. Antonio Rovira was a composer, organist and voice teacher from Cataluña who wrote orchestral works and zarzuelas. The confusion between the two musicians has also been complicated by the spelling of the name as "Robira," which could mean Rovira misspelled with a b or Rubira misspelled with an o. For more on Rovira, see bibliography entries for Saldoni pp. 48, 99, 178, 282, 283 and Suarez-Pajares p. 457.

5. The Spanish guitarists from the "post-Sor" era who visited or immigrated to the Rio de la Plata included not only Juan Valler and Antonio Rubira (who visited in a prolonged sojourn from 1881 to 1884), but also Gaspar Sagreras (1838-1901) and Bernardo Troncoso (1835-1928), who came in 1869; Carlos García Tolsa (1858-1905) in 1885; Pedro Maza (1870-1939) in 1889; Juan Crusans (1858-1905) in 1890; Antonio Jiménez Manjón in 1893 and Domingo Prat (1886-1944) in 1908. If the *Romance* was known in Spain via an oral tradition in the latter half of the 19th century, then it is perhaps not unreasonable to assume that many of these guitarists knew the piece and utilized it in their teaching.

6. An announcement dated August 14, 1872 in the Madrid newspaper *La Esperanza* states that "A new publication of music for guitar by accredited authors under the direction of D. Antonio Rubira is beginning to see the light of day. This publication will consist of monthly issues that contain a work from an opera correctly written and perfectly arranged, plus one original work. Solicitation for subscriptions can be made to the author, remitting the sum of 30 *reales* per trimester in Lorca (Múrcia)."

7. Herrera lists 41 editions of the work that have appeared in the 20th century.

8. In this movie French filmmaker Rene Clement featured only the guitar playing of Narciso Yepes for the soundtrack. In addition to the *Romance*, music by DeVisee, Rameau and Llobet was also used. The other movie in which the *Romance* was utilized was the 1941 film *Blood and Sand*, which featured the guitar playing of Vicente Gomez (who appears on camera in several scenes). The *Romance* melody in this film was used as the major "love theme" between the protagonists, and as such appears and reappears with numerous instrumental settings and harmonic treatments, even as a lyric operatic serenade-all created by the legendary film composer Alfred Newman (1901-1970).

BIBLIOGRAPHY

De Kloe, Jan: *Index of the Diccionario de Guitarristas by Domingo Prat*, Editions Orpheé, 2000.

Diccionario de la música española e hispanoamericana Volume 9, 2002: Sobrino, Ramón, "Antonio Rovira" pp. 441-442; Suarez-Pájares, Javier, "Antonio Rubira," p. 457.

Herrera, Francisco: *Enciclopedia de la Guitarra*, editada por Mariel Weber y Vincenzo Pocci, VP Musica ediciones, Roma 2001, "Antonio Rubira, Siglo XIX," pp. 2295-2297; "Jack Silver," pp. 2-29/30.

Herrera, Francisco: *Romance Anónimo-Melodia de Sor* (Siglo XIX), Piles Editorial, Valencia, Spain 1996.

Hii, Philip: "Estudio para guitarra por Antonio Rubira" on http://philiphii.com/2012/06/estudio-para-guitarra-by-antonio-rubira/.

Llanes, Ricardo M.:*Historia de la calle Florida*, 3 volúmenes, Imprenta del Congreso de la Nación, Buenos Aires 1976, Tomo II, pp. 235 and 241.

Porras Álvarez, Santiago: "Qué (no) sabemos del Romance ¿Anónimo?" on www.guitarra.artepulsado.com: http://guitarra.artepulsado.com/guitarra/romance-anonimo.php#mnota22 also http://guitarra.artepulsado.com/foros.showthread.php?103-Qu%E9-(no)-sabemos-del-Romance-%BFAn%F3nimo-por-Santiago-Porras/page2

Osborne, Randy: *Annotations for the History of the Classical Guitar in Argentina 1822-2000.*

Prat, Domingo: *Diccionario biográfico, bibliográfico, histórico, critic, de guitarras, guitarristas*, Domingo Prat, Ed. Romero y Fernández, Buenos Aires, 1934, pp. 74, 126, 274, 297, 327

Saldoni Baltasar: *Diccionario biográfico-bibliográfico de efemérides de músicos españoles*, Madrid, 1880, Vol. 1 pg. 99, Vol. II pg. 383, Vol. III pg. 48, Vol. IV pg. 282.

Savio, Isaias, "O Mito do Estudo de Rovira" in *Violao e Mestres*, 1965. (Also published English translation in *Soundboard*, V. 14. #1, 1988 as "The Romance fo the 'Romance'").

Tezuka, Takeshi: "The Mystery of Guitar Masterpieces" series, "The Unsolved Romance Issue: Who Caused it?" *Gendai Guitar*, Vol. 46, issue 578 May 2012, pp. 56-57 and issue 579 June 2012, pp. 55-57.

Todotango.com: http://www.todotango.com/english/biblioteca/cronicas/Cronica_editoras2.asp

Viglietti, Cedar: *Origen e historia de la guitarra*, Editorial Albatros, Buenos Aires 1973.

Guitar by Richard Prenkert
K & K Trinity Mix Amplification
Strings by Hannabach

A special thank you to Julio Gimeno for his contribution.
My appreciation to Philip Hii and Keith Calmes.

Archives consulted from the collection of www.finefretted.com owner Randy Osborne (1949-): Mario Rodriguez Arenas (1879-1949), José Augusto Marcellino (1911-1970), Ricardo Muñoz (1887-1967) and Pedro Mascaro y Ressig (1888-1952).

A recording of the *Viuda de Aramburo* cylinder performance of the *Romance* by Simon Ramirez can be heard on Doremi Records CD "Segovia and His Contemporaries" Volume 12.

The *Romance* is the third most recorded original work for guitar according to Enrique Robichaud, author of the forthcoming book *Guitar's Top 100. Classical Guitar's Most Recorded Music* (ISBN 978-0-9881320-0-9).

Romance Anónimo Music Examples

The versions of the *Romance Anónimo* analyzed are all written in 3/4 meter with three distinct right hand fingering patterns and styles of calligraphy: aimi, aim and ami.

aimi: Medina e Hijo, Maza

aim: manuscript 1, Soares — Hernandez — manuscript 2

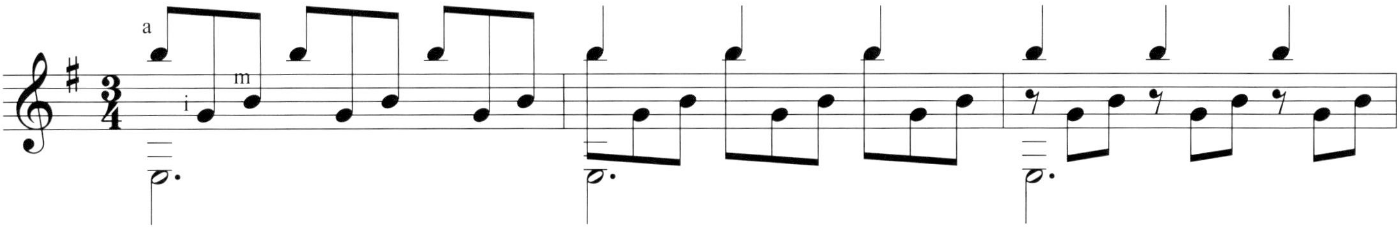

ami: Llobet, Yepes — Fortea, Gomez

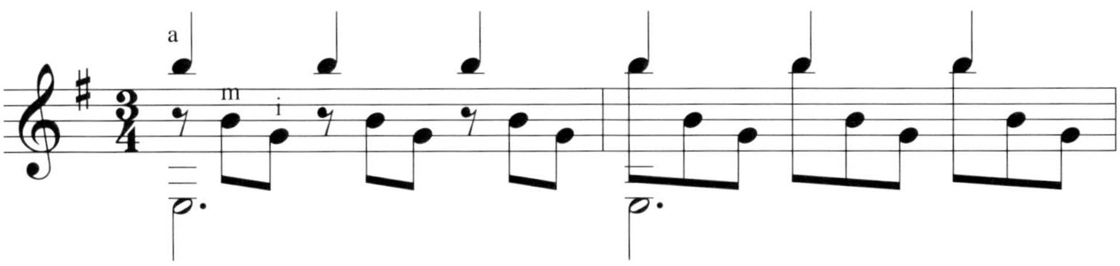

Slight musical differences are seen at measures 3, 4, 5, 6, 11-14, 19, 20, 29, 31.

measure 3: apoggiatura ornament on beat 1
J. A. Medina e Hijo, Pedro Maza

measure 4: a glissando in measure 4
Fortea, Llobet, Yepes (also in Medina & Soares)

measure 5: the same glissando notated with apoggiatura
manuscripts 1 & 2, Hernandez

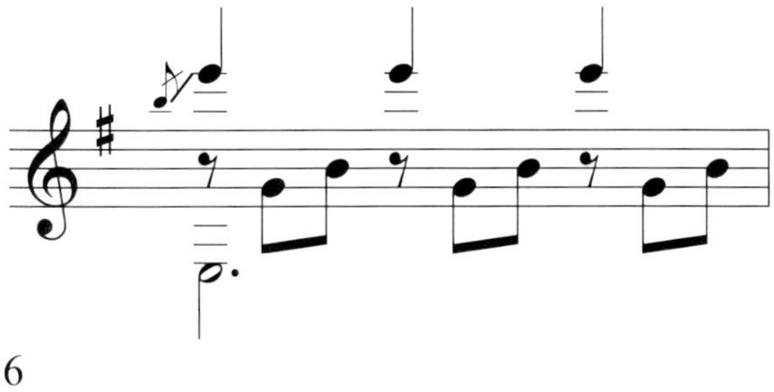

measure 6: Gomez

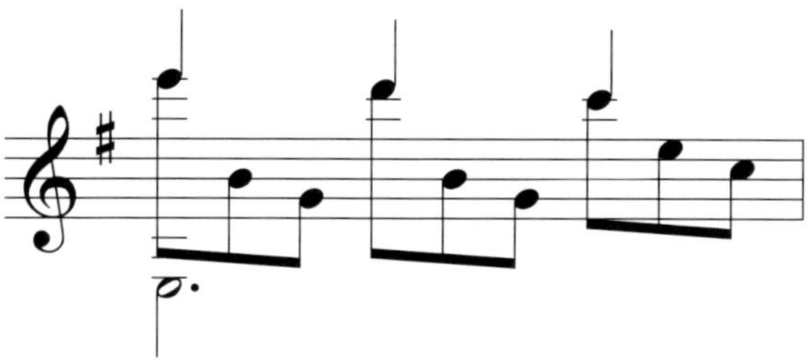

measures 11-14
J.A. Medina e Hijo, Pedro Maza

measure 14
Hernandez & Soares

Fortea, Gomez, Llobet, Yepes
(also both ms. with aim)

measure 19-20
manuscript 2, Hernandez, Soares (also Yepes with ami)

Fortea, Llobet (also manuscript 1 with aim)

Gomez

(The Medina bass line "mixes" ideas with f sharp at measure 19 and b at measure 20).

measure 29
Hernandez, both ms., Soares (also Fortea, Llobet, Medina & Yepes with ami)

measure 29
Gomez

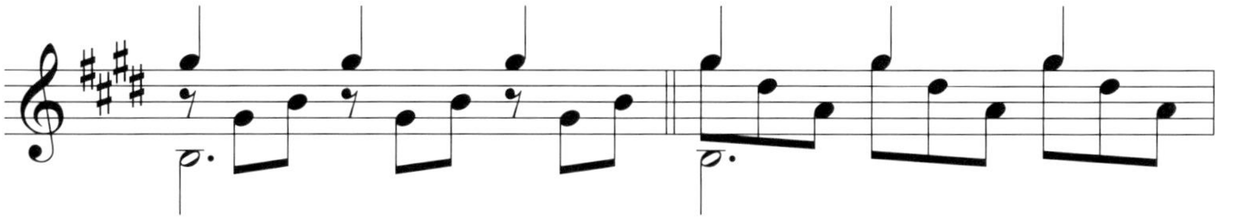

measure 31
Hernandez, both ms., Soares (also Fortea, Llobet, Medina & Yepes with ami)

measure 31
Gomez

measure 31
J.A. Medina e Hijo

measure 31
Pedro Maza

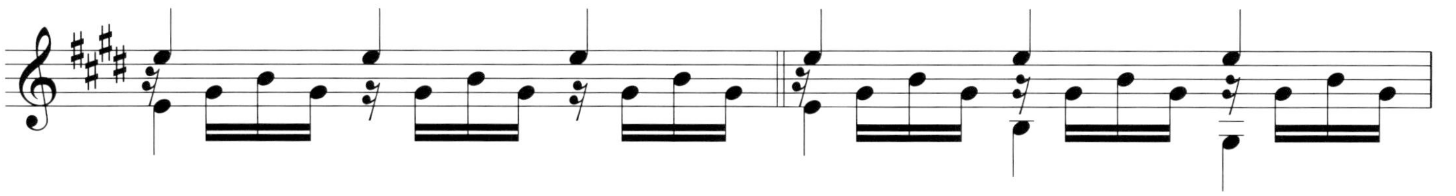

Reproduced on the following pages is the original edition of the work published circa 1900 by JA Medina e Hijo. This date is an interpolation based on plate numbers, magazine advertisements as well as the actual location of the firm, which on the cover of the edition shown here is listed as "119 Florida", the first of three different locales on Florida Street that the company occupied during its nearly five decades of existence. As noted above, it is quite probable that this edition with plate no. 23697 dates from even before 1900.

The fact that the name Rovira is shown here instead of Rubira is interesting in that it would seem to indicate that Rubira himself did not do this edition (as it seems illogical that he would edit it with his name misspelled). Chronologically this is the earliest appearance of the name "Rovira" as the composer, a mix-up that has clouded the picture ever since. Also unusual about this version are the melodic differences noted in measures 11 through 14 as well as the a-i-m-i fingering (which gives it a Giuliani-like quality).

ESTUDIO para GUITARRA

Rovira

Prop. del Editor J. A. MEDINA e hijo

ESTUDIO
PARA
GUITARRA
por
ROVIRA
Nº 23697
EDICION
J. A. MEDINA é HIJO
119 FLORIDA 119